NOTE-FOR-NOTE TRANSCRIPTIONS • FROM THE ORIGINAL RECORDINGS

transcribed **Horns**

JAZZ/POP
HORN SECTION

CONTENTS

Transcribed by Forrest "Woody" Mankowski

ISBN 978-1-61780-473-1

HAL•LEONARD®
CORPORATION

7777 W. BLUEMOUND RD. P.O. BOX 13819 MILWAUKEE, WI 53213

Visit Hal Leonard Online at
www.halleonard.com

AFTER THE LOVE HAS GONE

Words and Music by DAVID FOSTER,
JAY GRAYDON and BILL CHAMPLIN

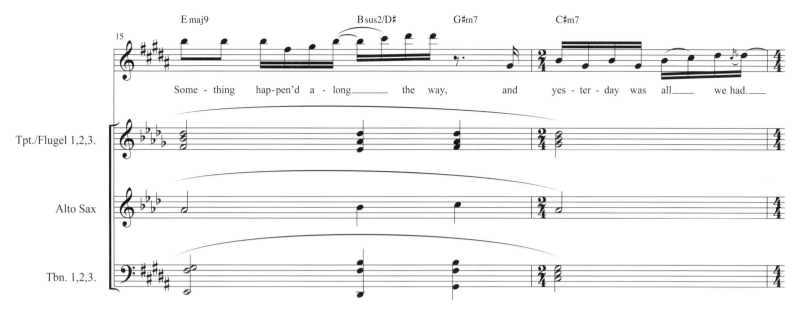

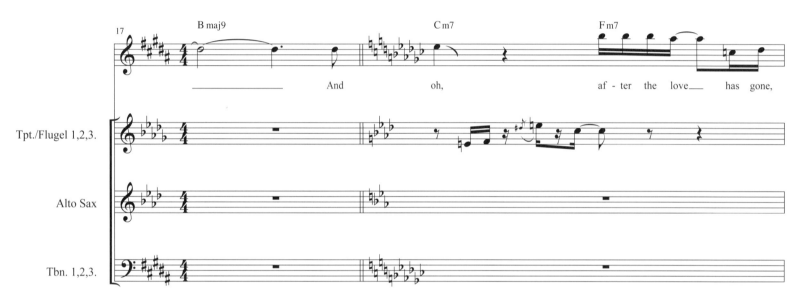

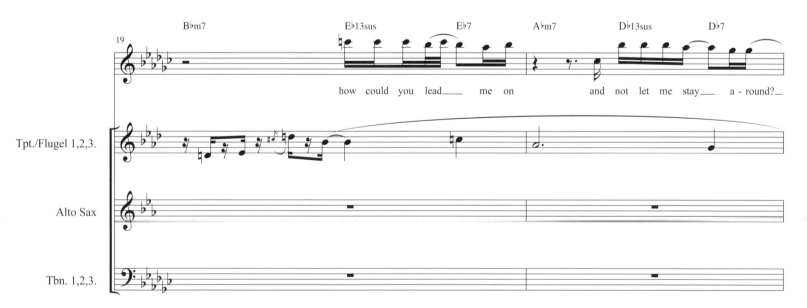

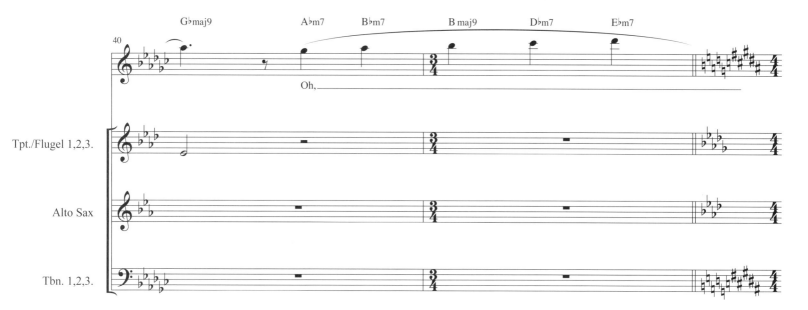

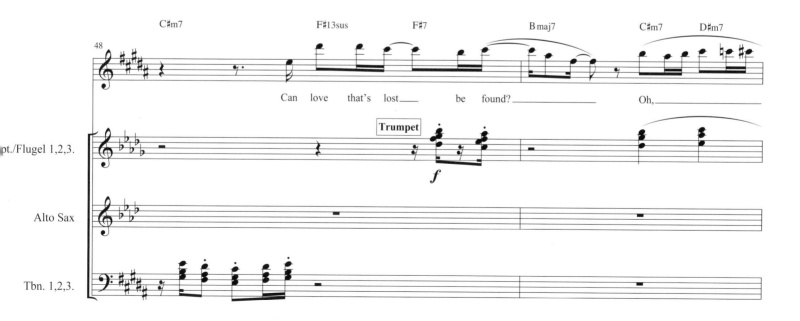

Additional lyrics:

2. For awhile to love each other was all
we would ever need.
Love was strong for so long,
never knew that what was
wrong, oh baby, wasn't right.
We tried to find what we had,
'til sadness was all we shared.
We were scared this affair would lead our love into.
Somethin' happened along the way
yesterday was all we had.
Somethin' happened along the way
what used to be happy is sad.

To *Chorus*

BIRDLAND

By JOSEF ZAWINUL

14

21

Tenor Sax Solo

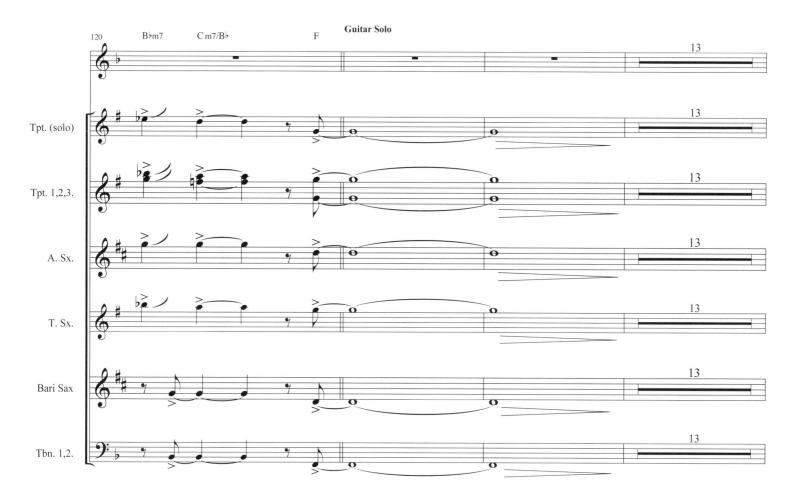

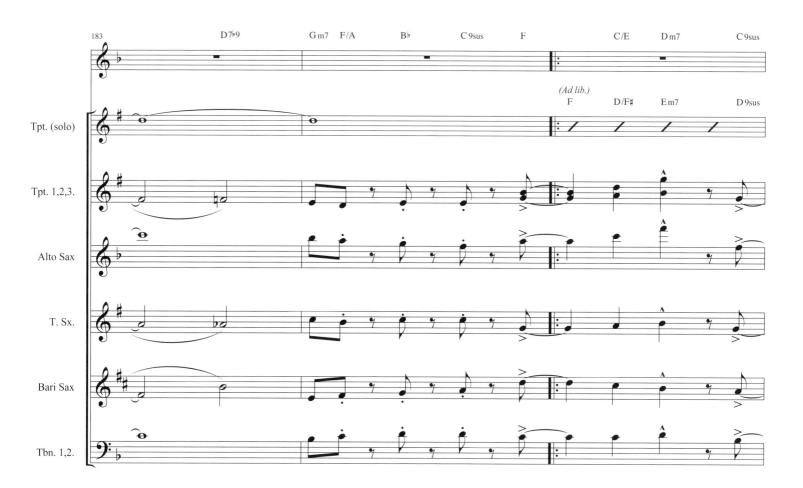

32

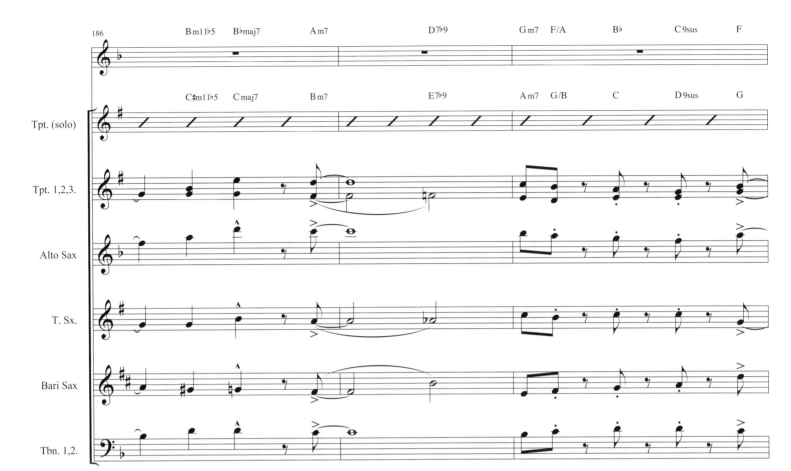

Play 6 Times and Fade

DEACON BLUES

Words and Music by WALTER BECKER
and DONALD FAGEN

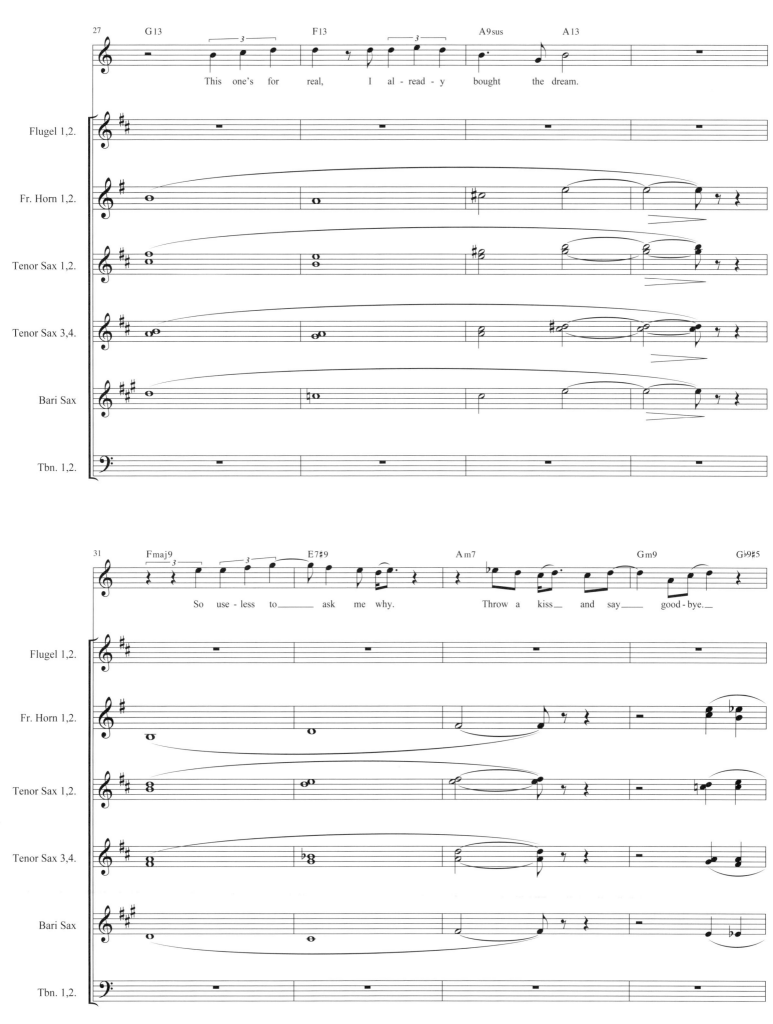

To Coda

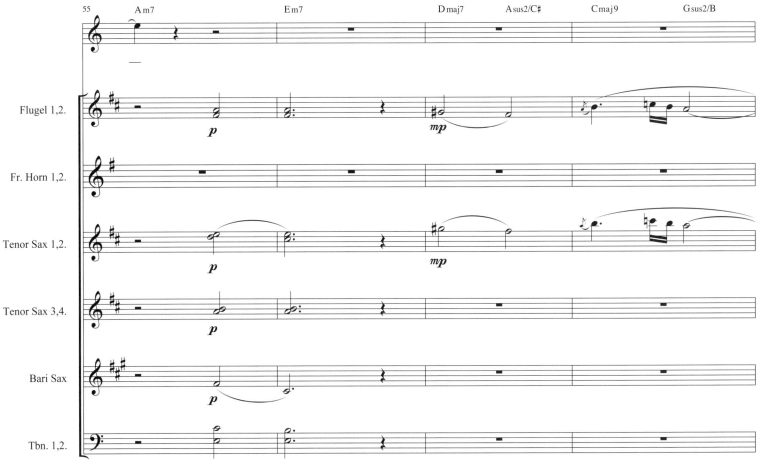

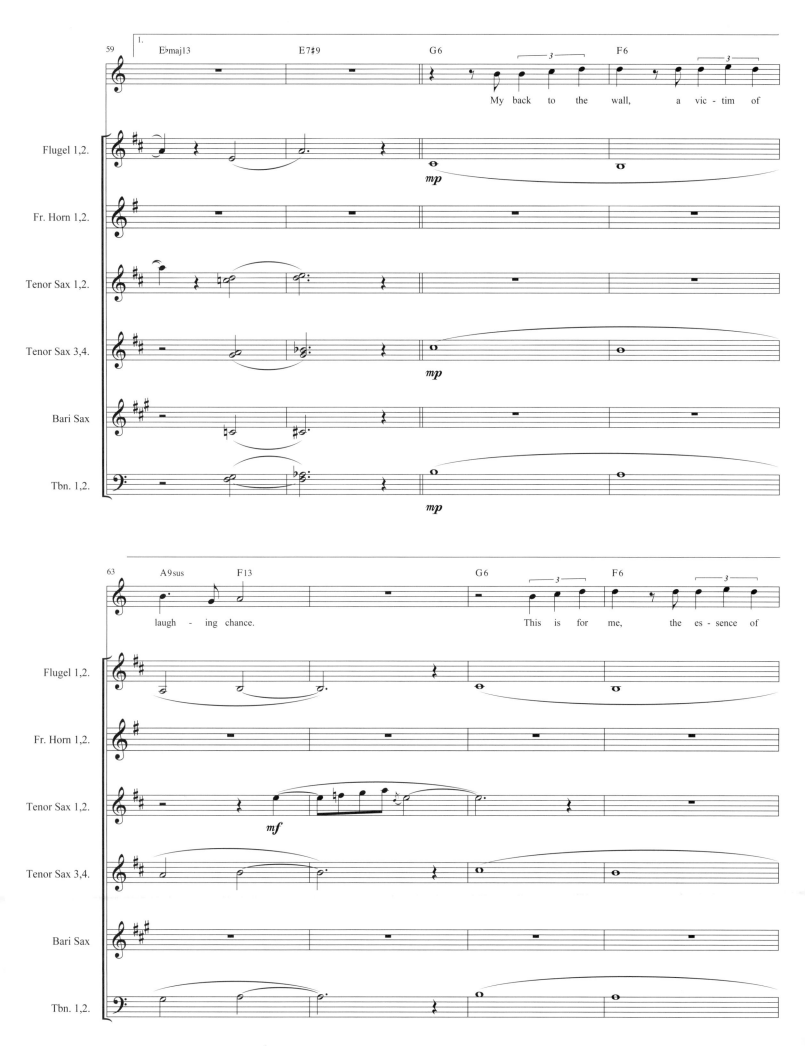

I'll make it my home sweet home.
I'll be what I want to be.

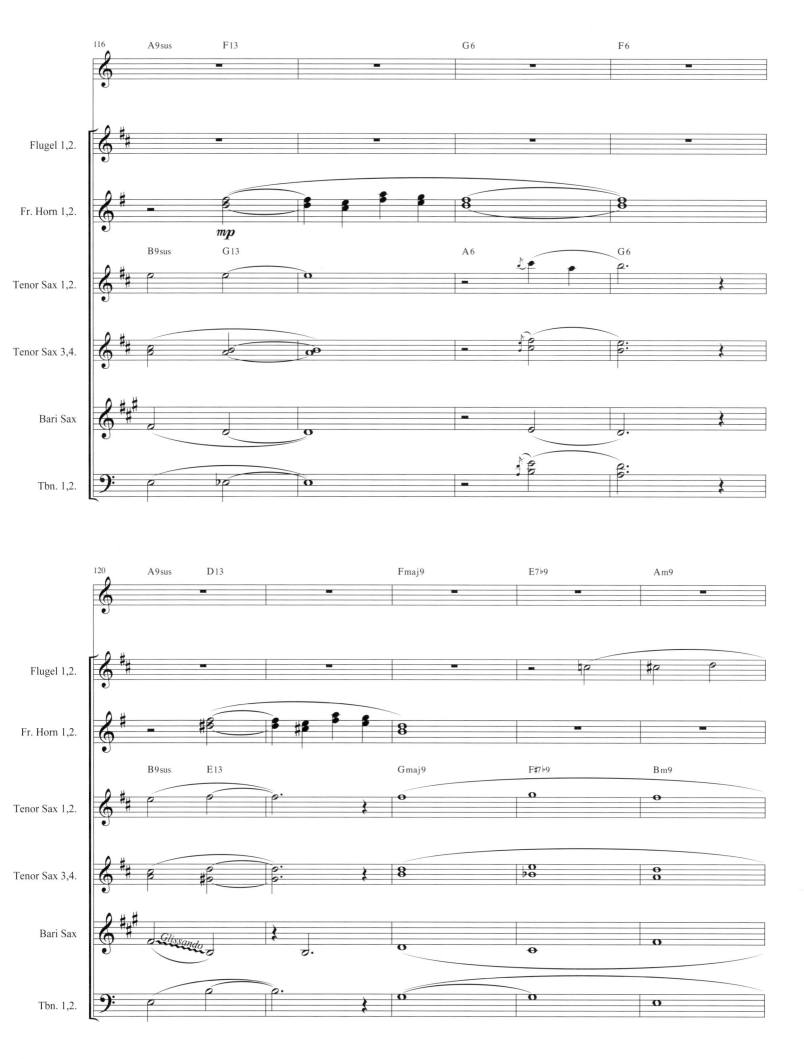

48

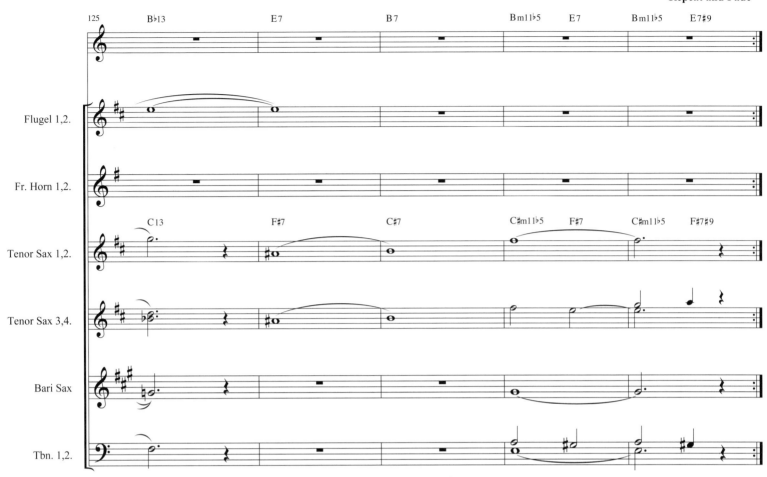

Repeat and Fade

DOIN' IT (ALL FOR MY BABY)

Words and Music by PHIL CODY
and MIKE DUKE

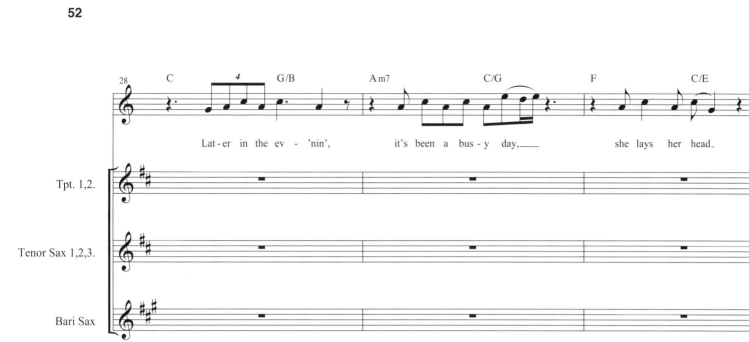

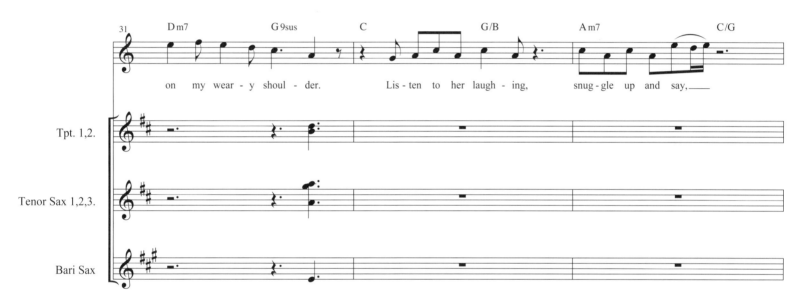

Do - in' it, do - in' it, ooh, hoo,____ hoo.____ Do - in' it all for my
(Lead vocal ad lib.)

ba - by. Do - in' it all for my ba - by.

Repeat and Fade

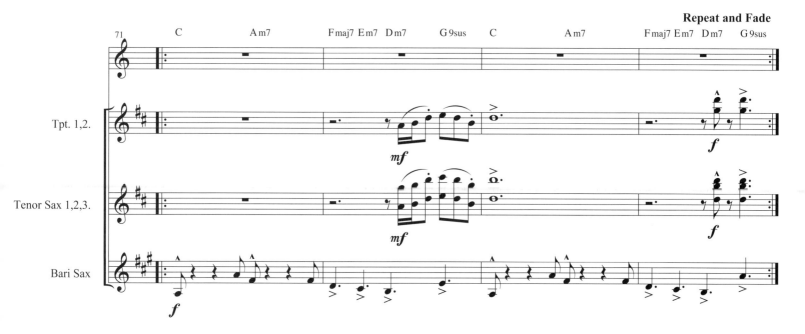

FANTASY

Words and Music by MAURICE WHITE,
VERDINE WHITE and EDDIE DEL BARRIO

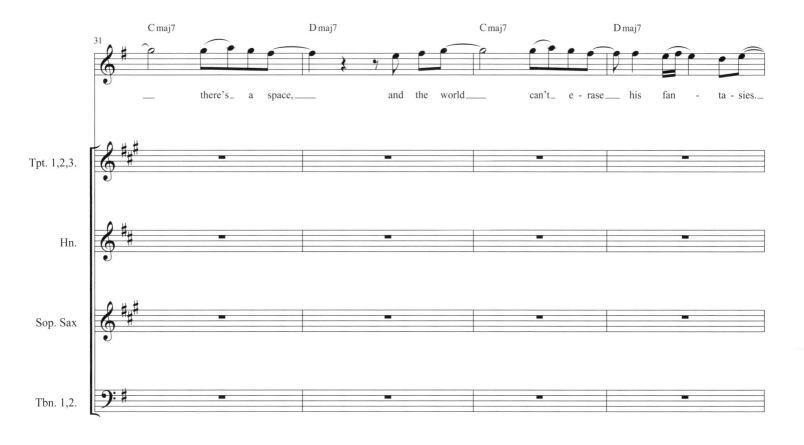

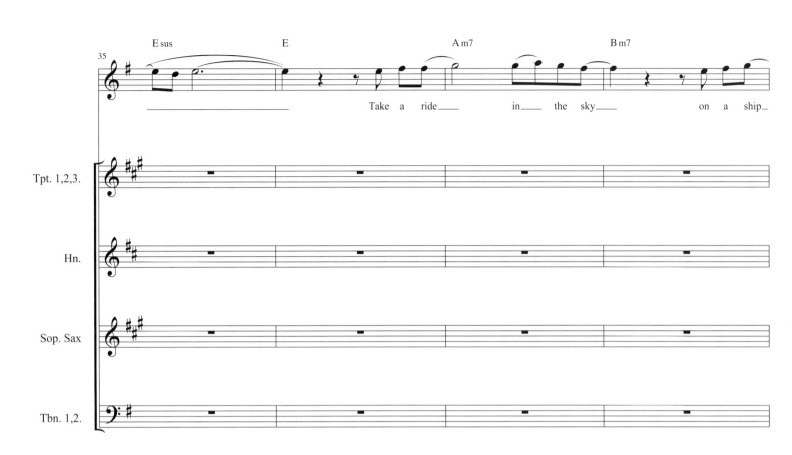

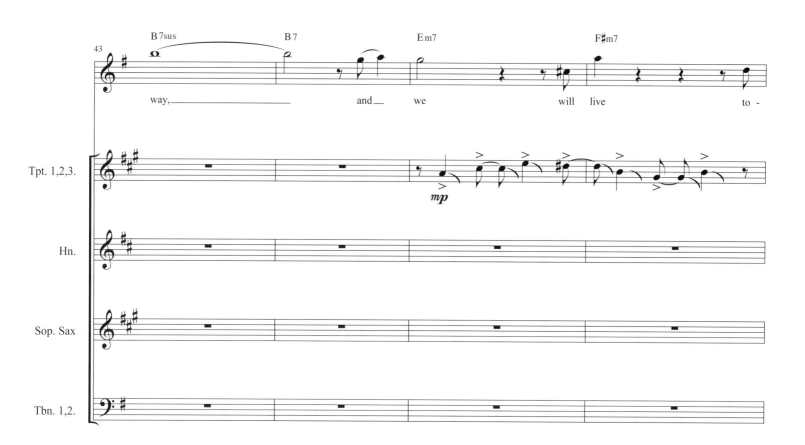

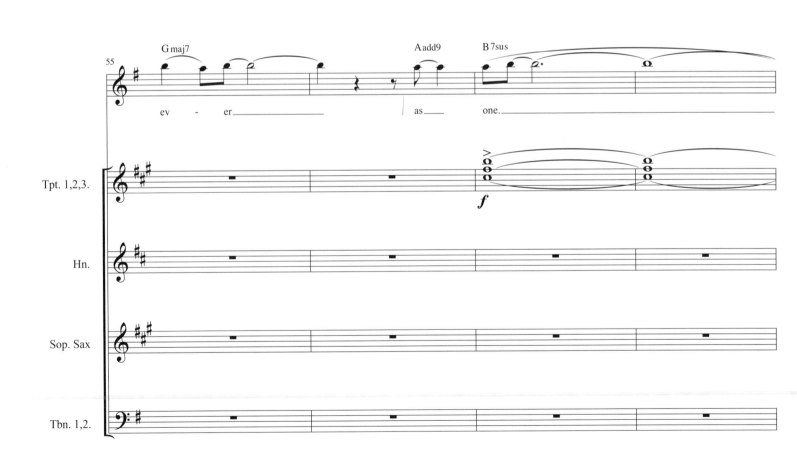

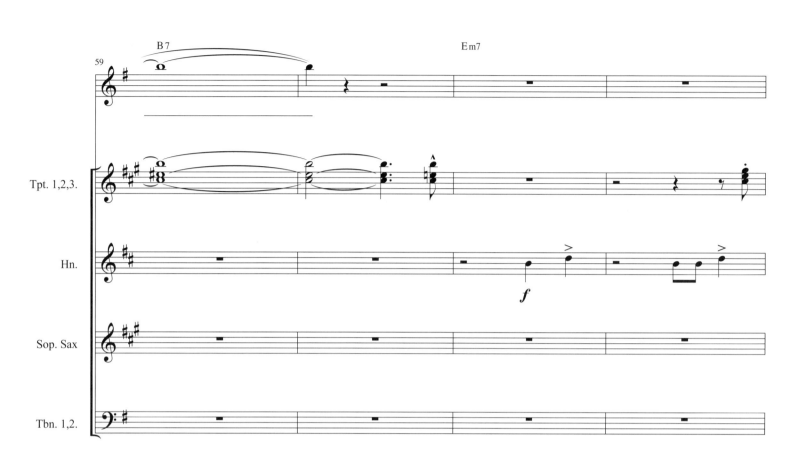

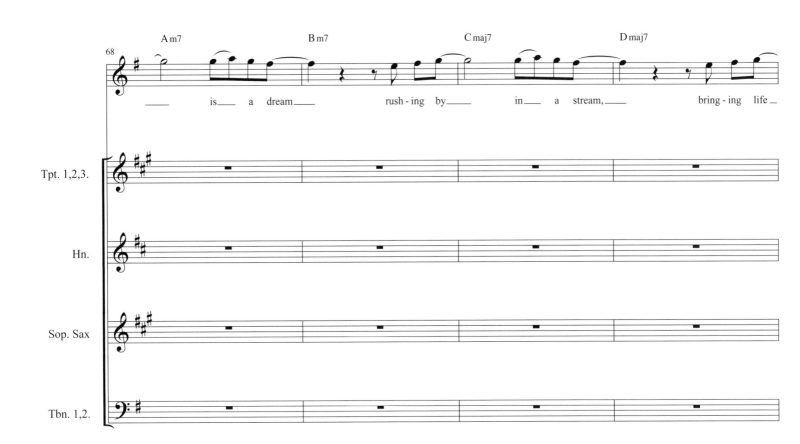

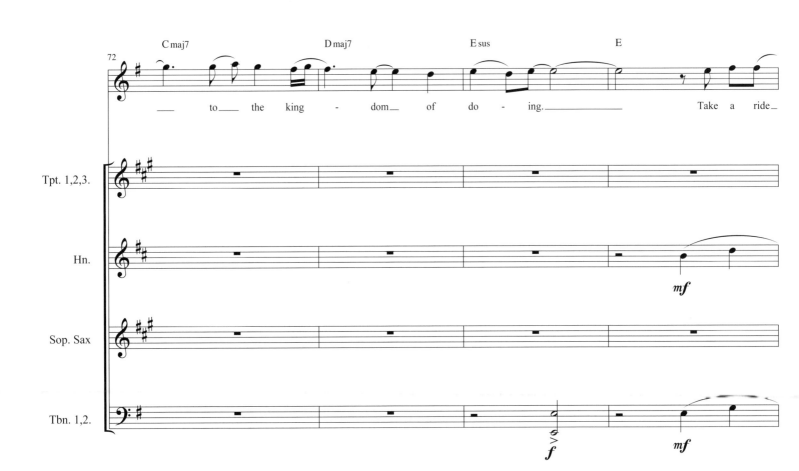

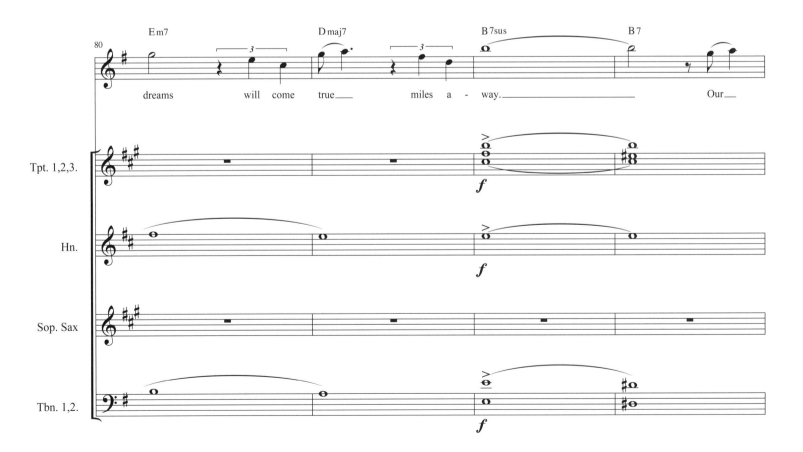

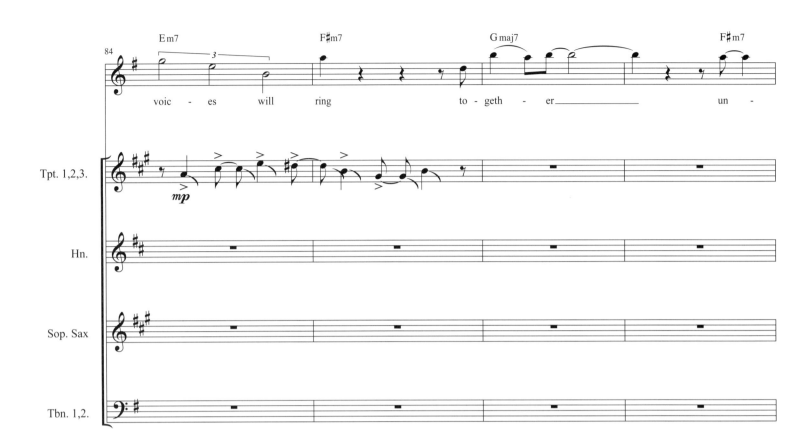

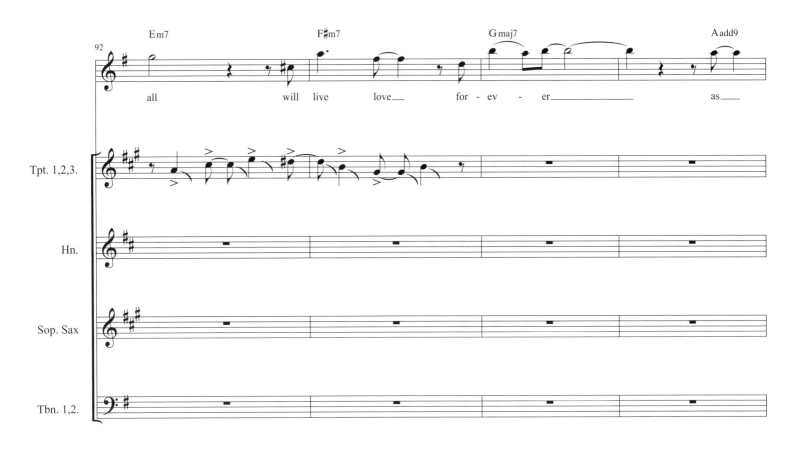

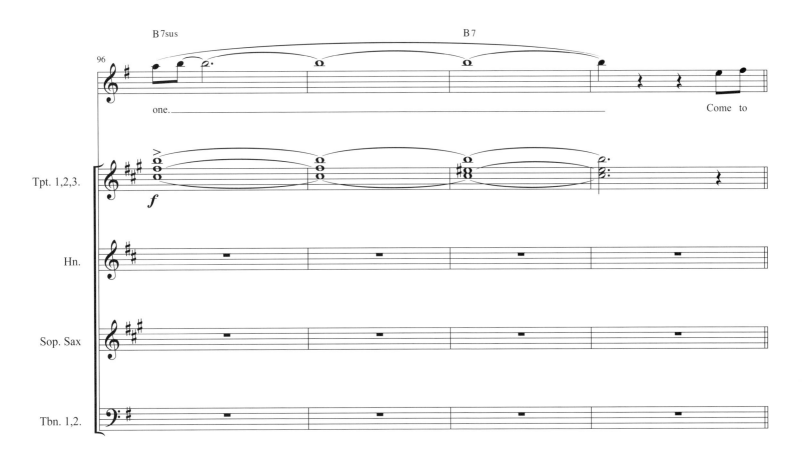

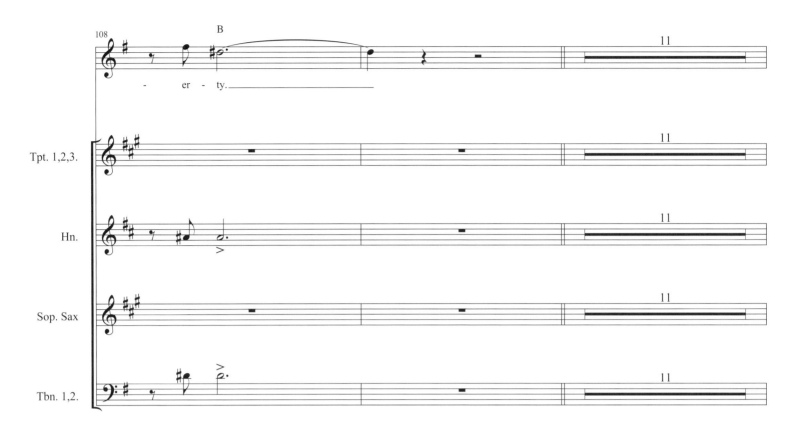

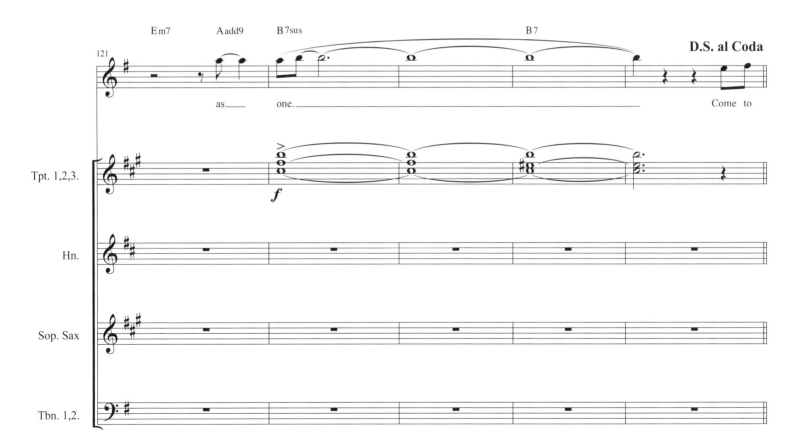

Coda

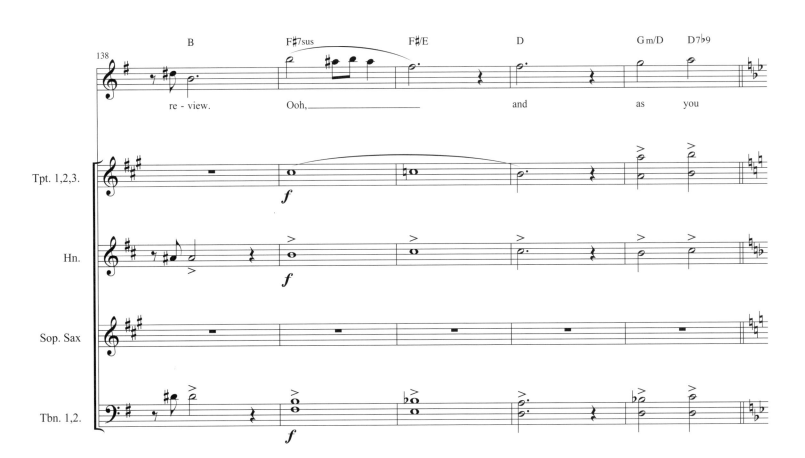

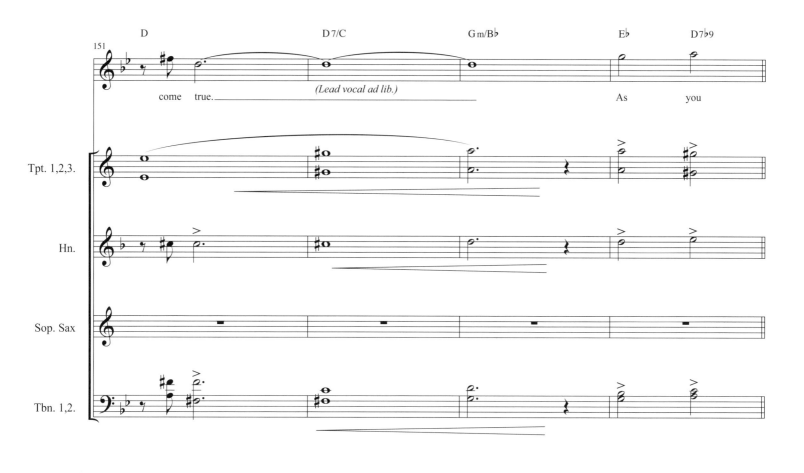

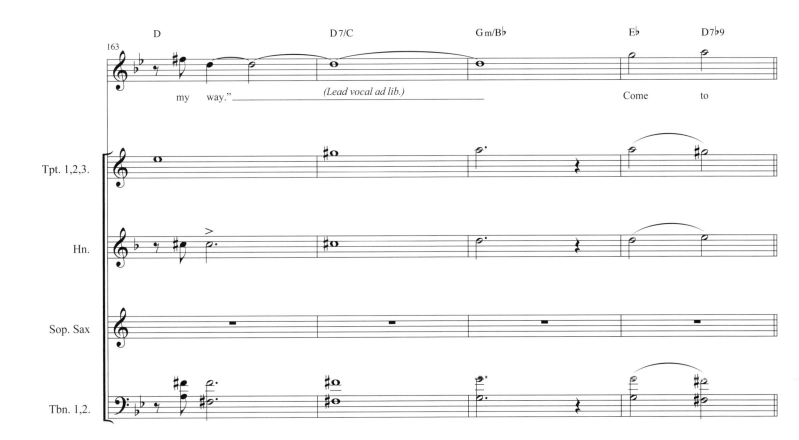

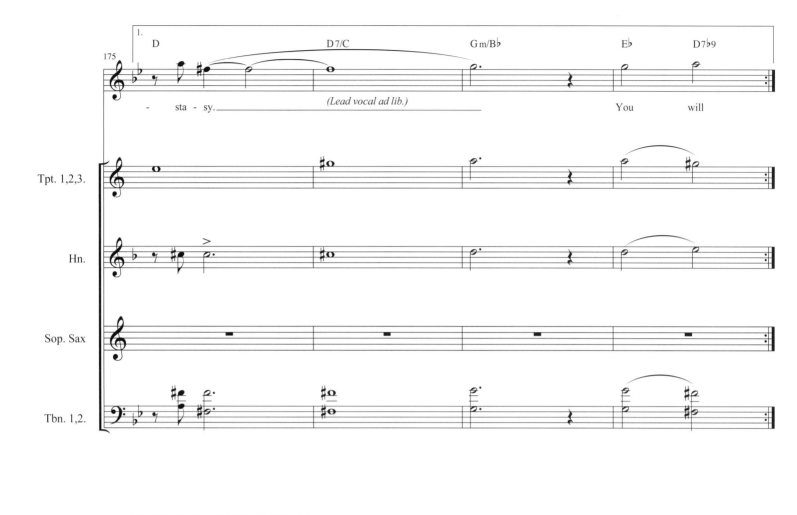

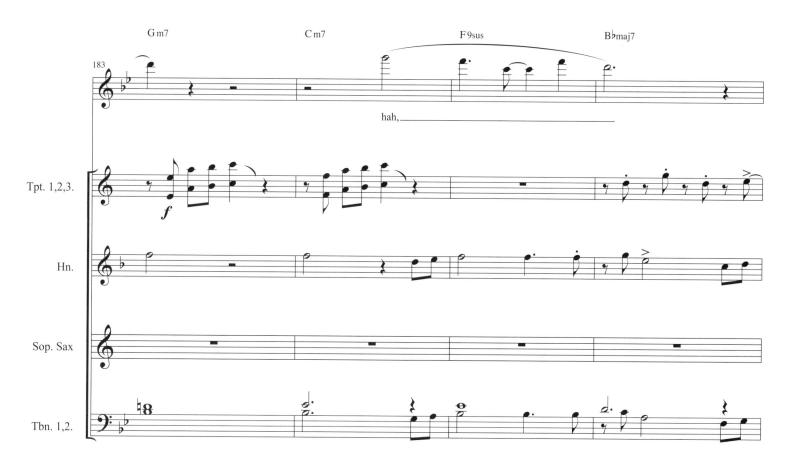

GOT TO GET YOU INTO MY LIFE

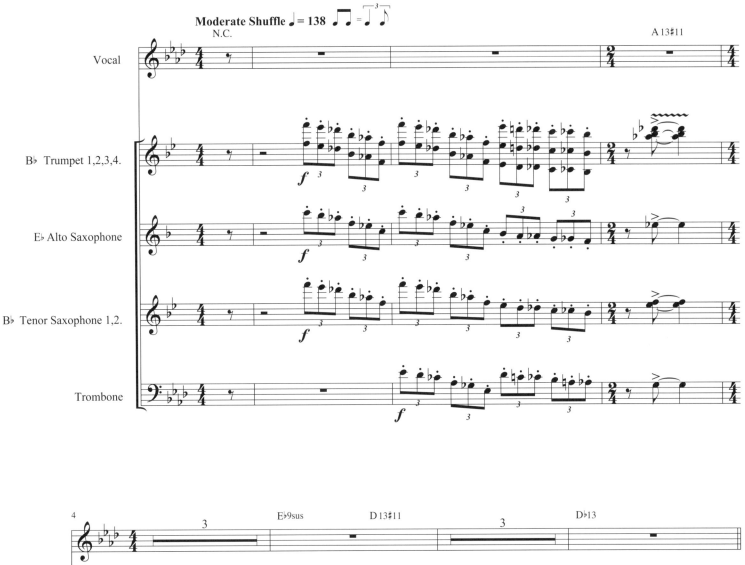

Words and Music by JOHN LENNON
and PAUL McCARTNEY

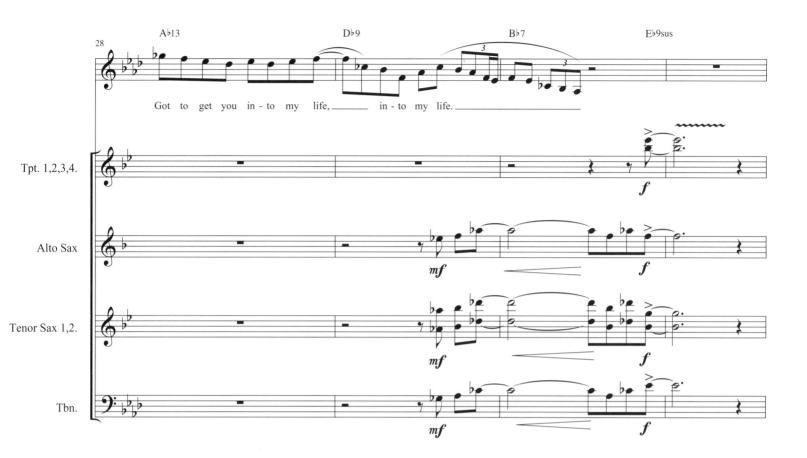

Got to get you in - to my life, _____ in - to my life. _____

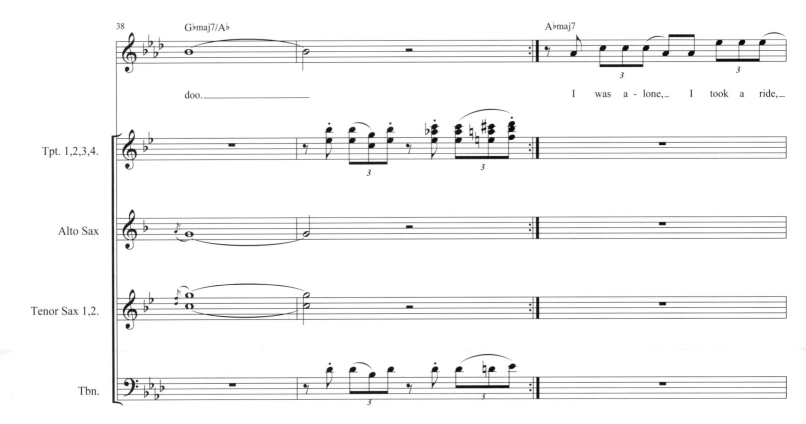

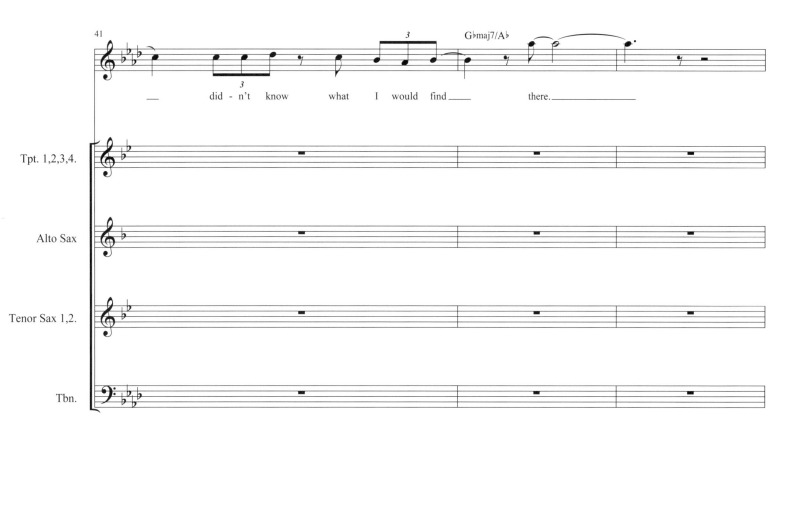

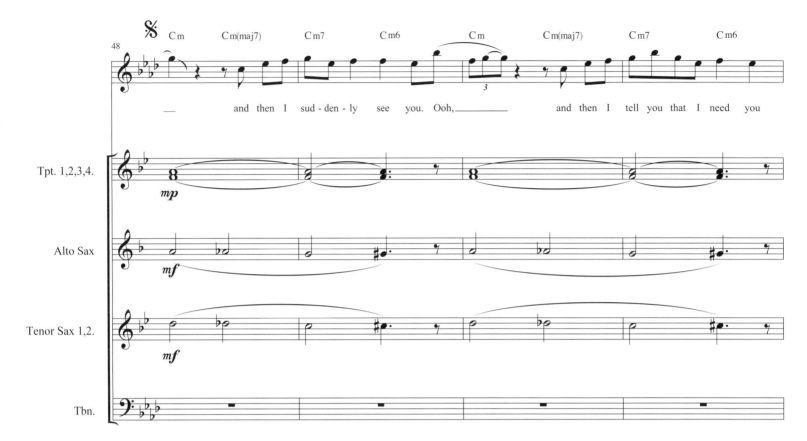

To Coda ⊕

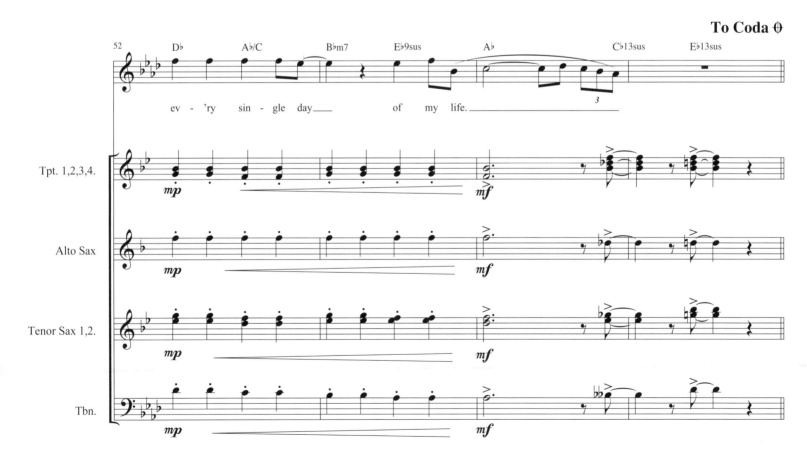

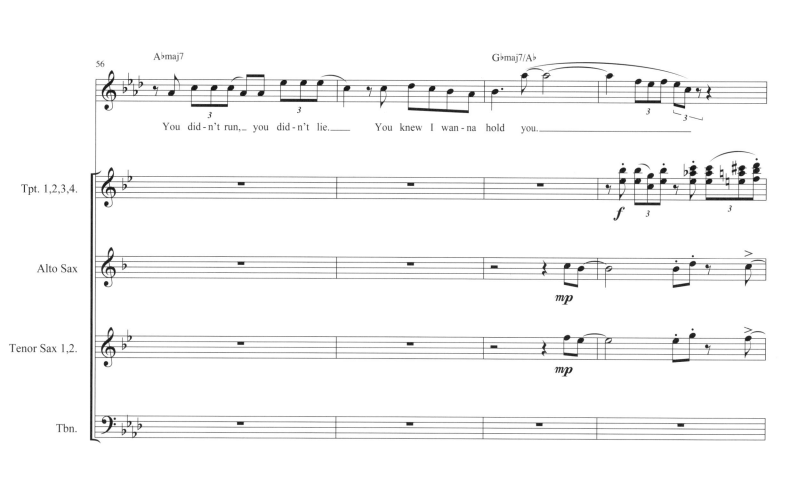

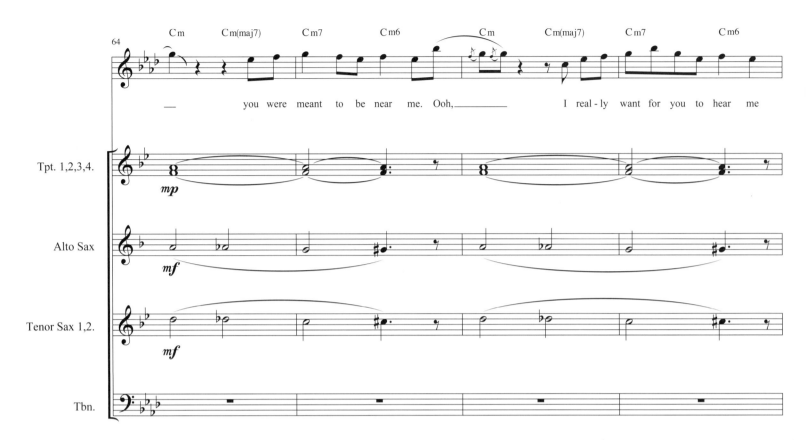

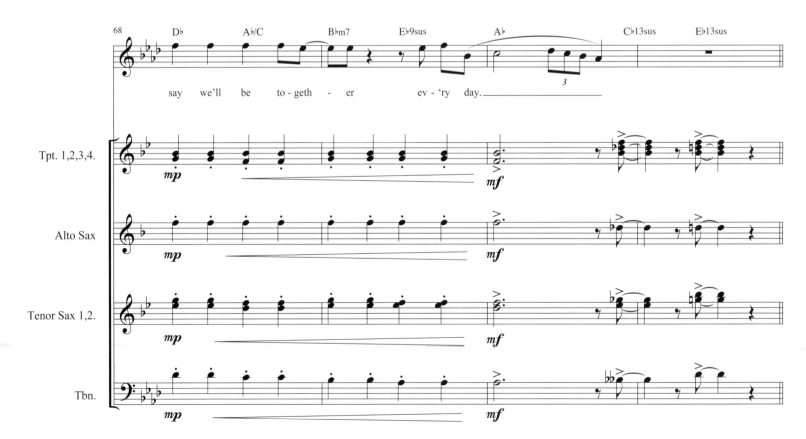

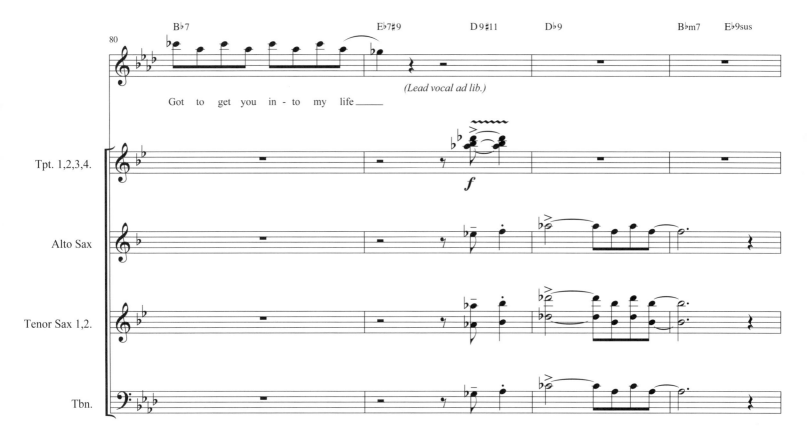

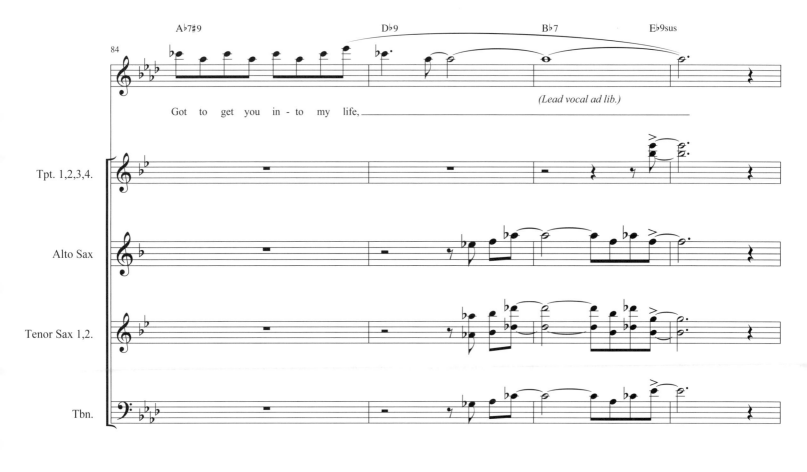

92

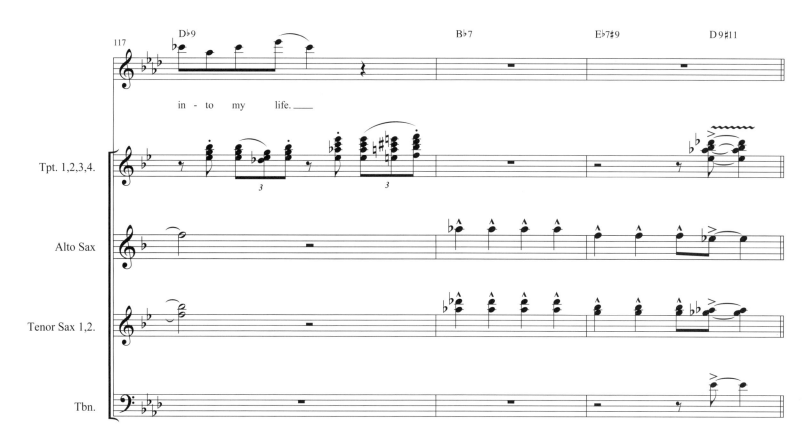

GRAZING IN THE GRASS

Words by HARRY ELSTON
Music by PHILEMON HOU

96

IN THE NAVY

Words and Music by JACQUES MORALI,
HENRI BELOLO and VICTOR WILLIS

Where can you find plea - sure, search_
If you like ad - ven - ture, don't_

_ the world for trea - sure, learn sci - ence, tech - nol - o - gy?_____
_ you wait to en - ter the re - cruit - ing of - fice fast._____

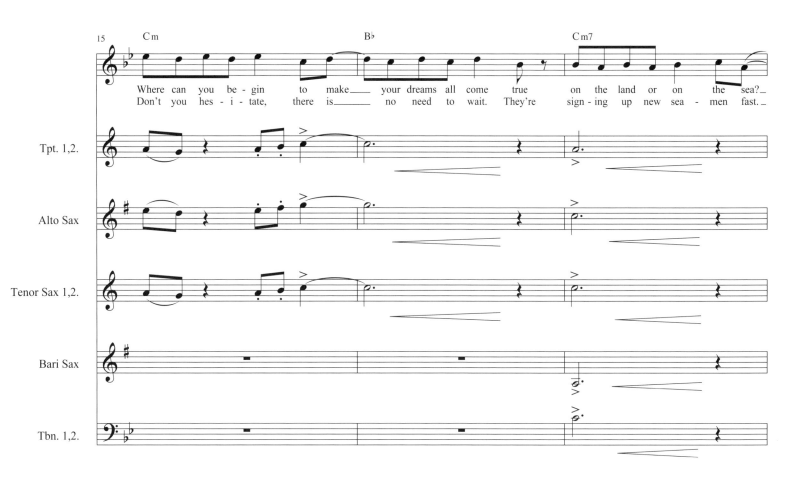

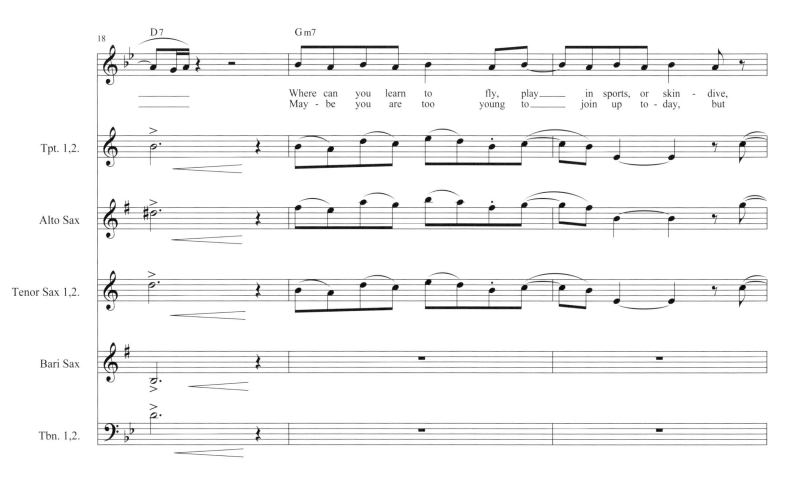

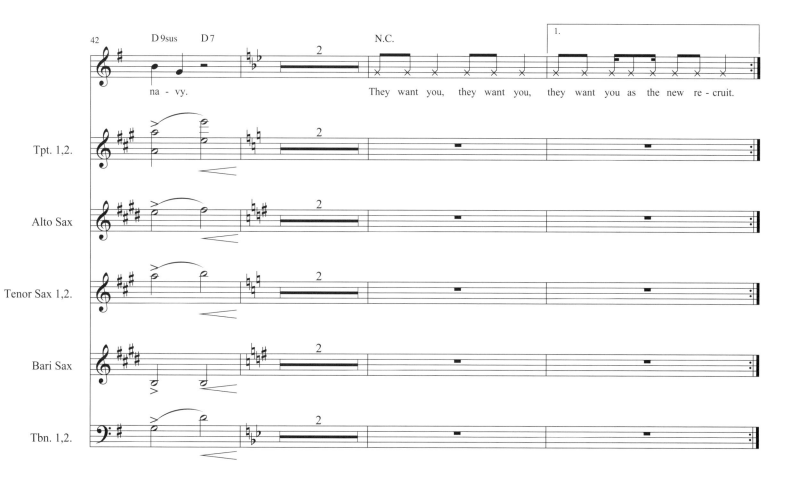

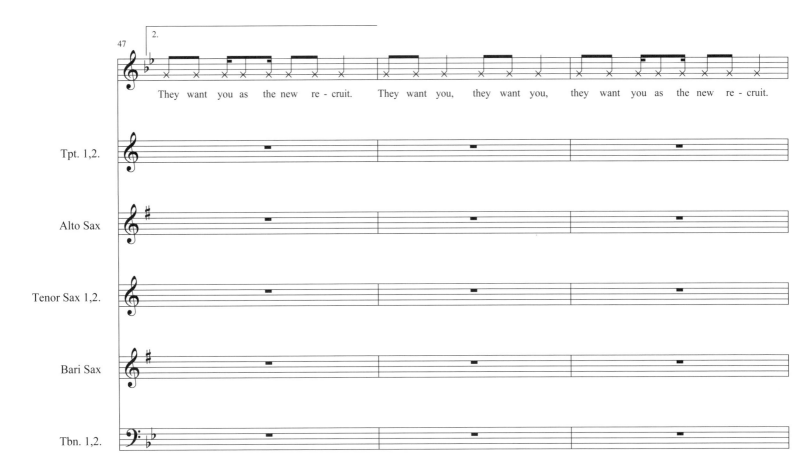

They want you as the new re-cruit. They want you, they want you, they want you as the new re-cruit.

G m7

(Lead vocal ad lib.)

THE MADISON TIME

Words by EDDIE MORRISON
Music by RAY BRYANT

Spoken Lyrics

It's Madison time. Hit it!

1. You're lookin' good. A big strong line.
   When I say "hit it", I want you to go two up and two back
   with a big strong turn, and back to the Madison.
   Hit-ta! You're lookin' good.

2. Now when I say "hit it", I want you to go two up and two back,
   Double-cross, come out of it with the Rifleman.
   Hit-ta!
   Crazy!

3. Now when I say "hit it", I want the strong "M",
   Erase it, and back to the Madison.
   Hit it!
   Walk on. You're lookin' good.

4. Now then, when I say "hit it", it'll be "T" time.
   Hit it!
   Big strong line.

5. Now when I say "hit it", I want the big strong Cleveland Box,
   And back to the Madison.
   Hit it! Crazy!

6. Now when I say "hit it",
   I want the big strong Basketball
   with the Wilt Chamberlain hook.
   Hit it! Two points!
   Now this time when I say hit it,
   I want the big strong Jackie Gleason,
   And back to the Madison.

7. Hit it! And away we go.
   Now then, when I say "hit it", Birdland 'til I say stop.
   Hit it! How 'bout a little stiff leg there?
   You're lookin' good.

8. Now when I say "hit it", come out of the Birdland, back to the Madison.
   Hit it! Crazy!
   When I say "hit it", go two up and two back, double-cross and freeze.
   Hit it!
   And hold it right there.

MY OLD SCHOOL

Words and Music by WALTER BECKER
and DONALD FAGEN

122

SPANISH FLEA

Words and Music by
JULIUS WECHTER

The chord symbols in this song are in concert pitch.

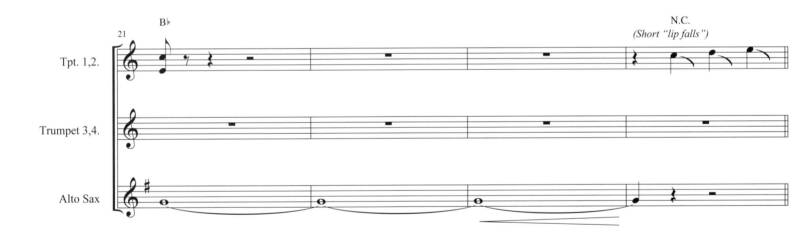

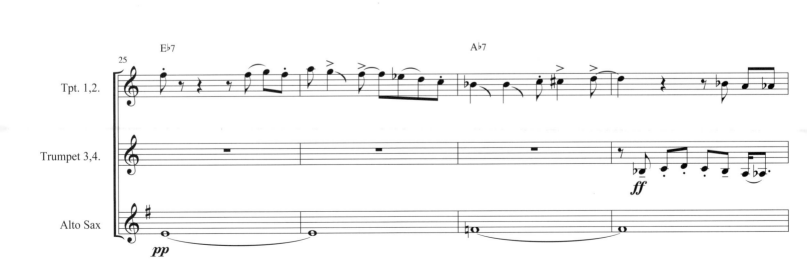

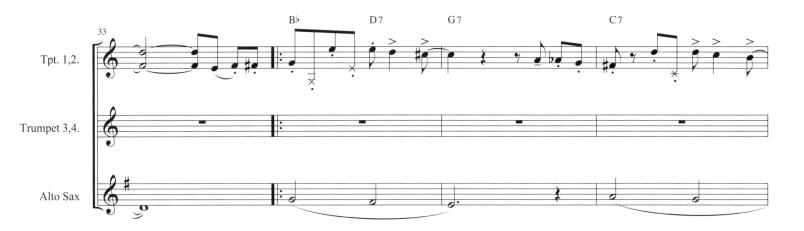

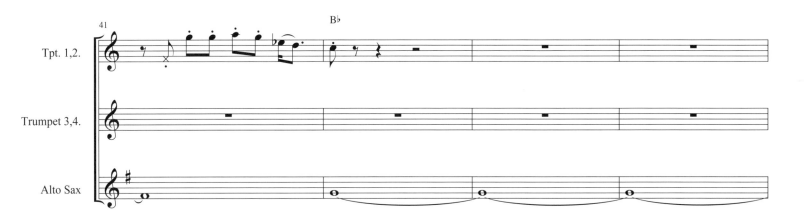

TELL HER ABOUT IT

Words and Music by
BILLY JOEL

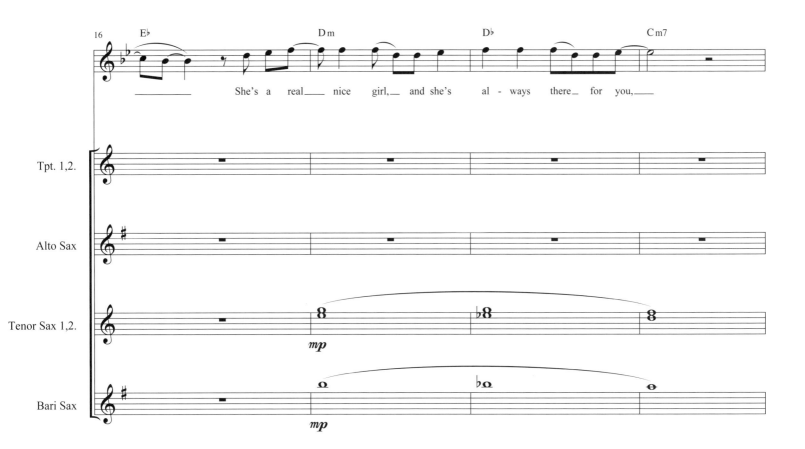

She's a real___ nice girl,___ and she's al - ways there___ for you,___

but a nice___ girl would-n't tell___ you what___ you should do.___

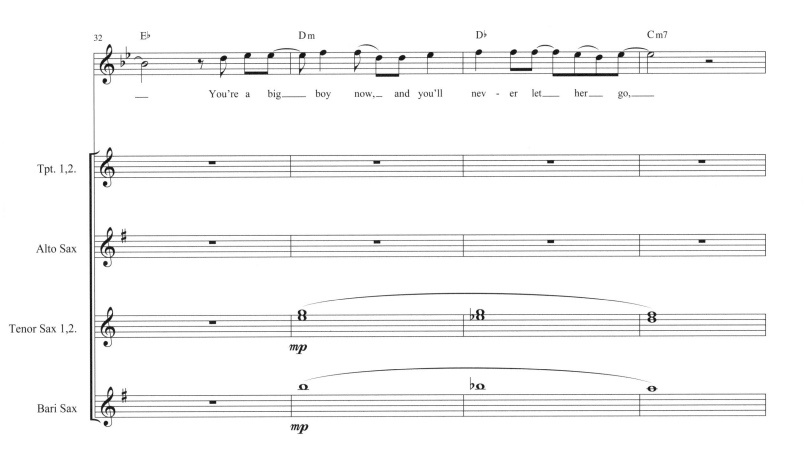

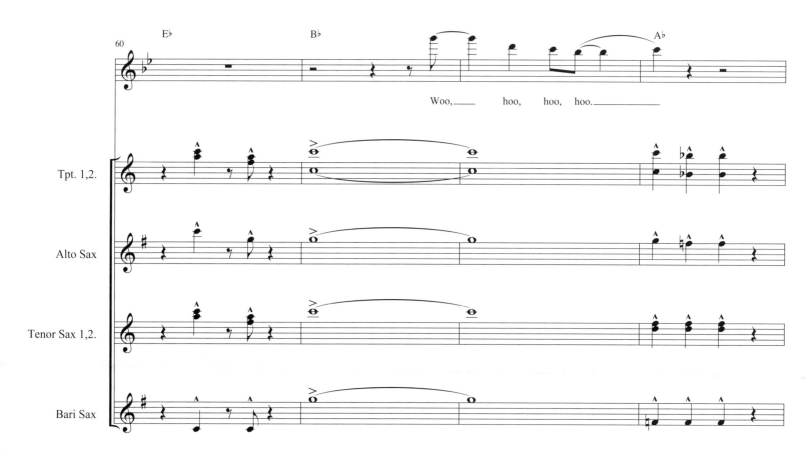

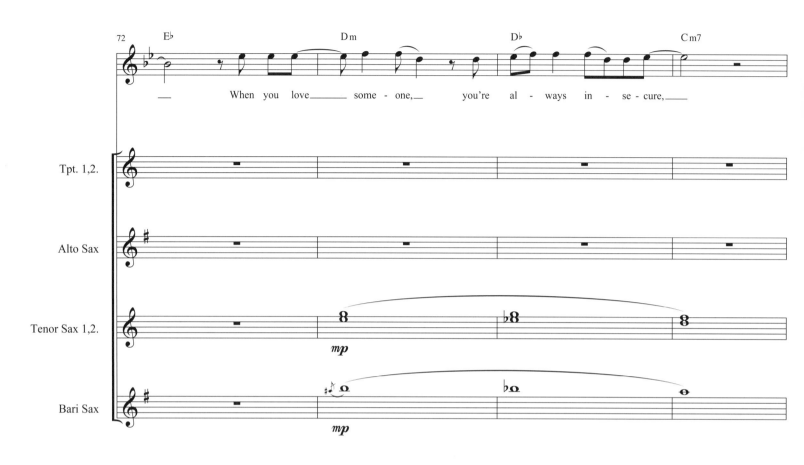

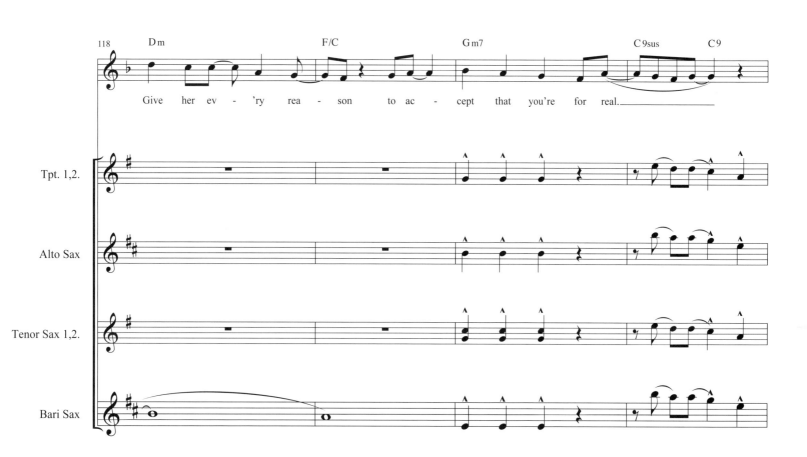

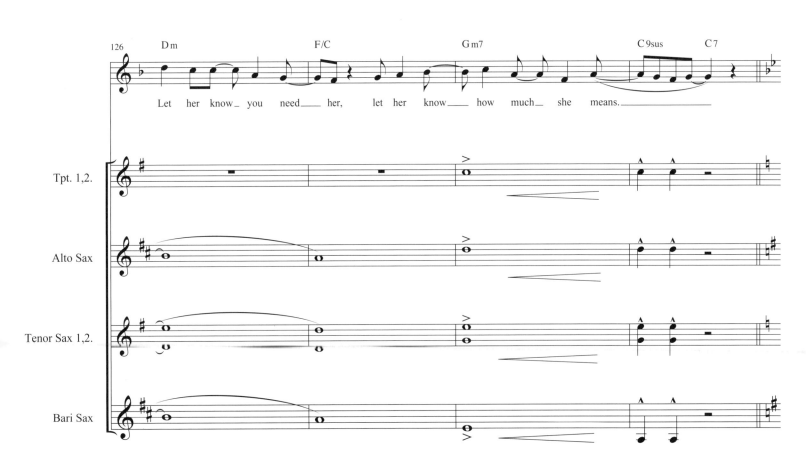

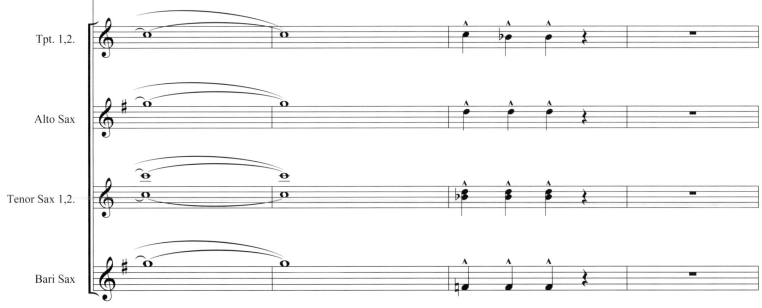

Repeat and Fade

tell   her a - bout___ it.   You got - ta tell,   tell,   tell___ her a - bout__ it, now.

TIJUANA TAXI

Words by JOHNNY FLAMINGO
Music by ERVAN "BUD" COLEMAN

* The chord symbols in this song are concert pitched.

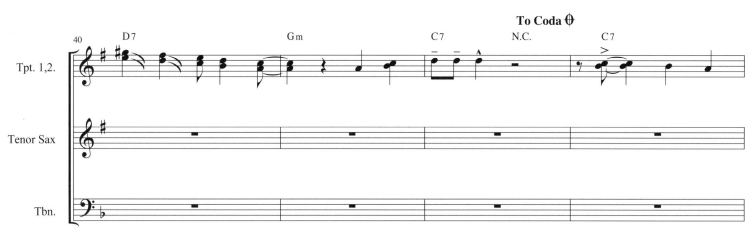

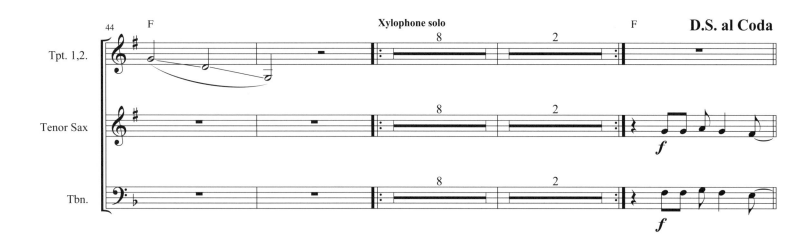

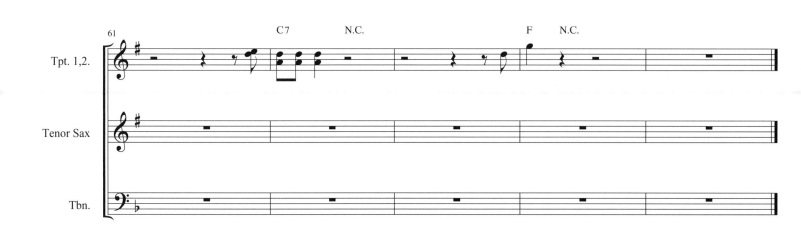

WHAT YOU WON'T DO FOR LOVE

Words and Music by BOBBY CALDWELL
and ALFONS KETTNER

I searched_ to find_ a love_ with-in.____ And I___ came back_ to let___ you know,_

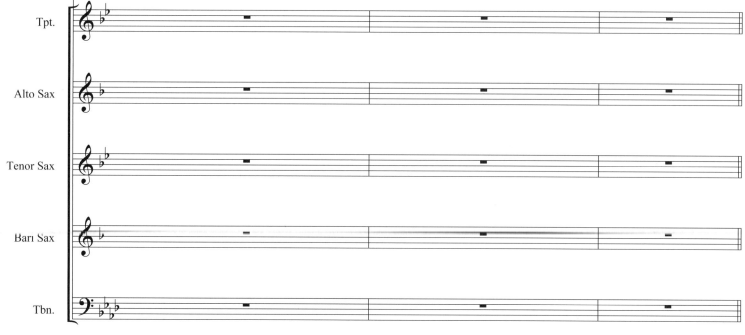

____ 'got a thing___ for you,_ and I can't_ let_ go.___

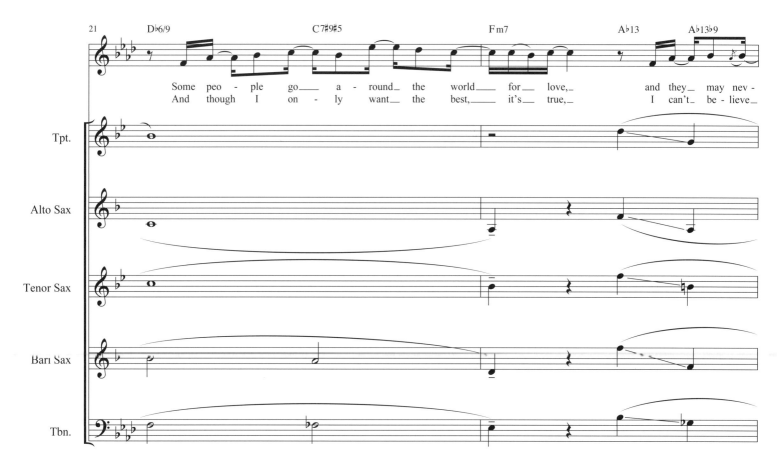

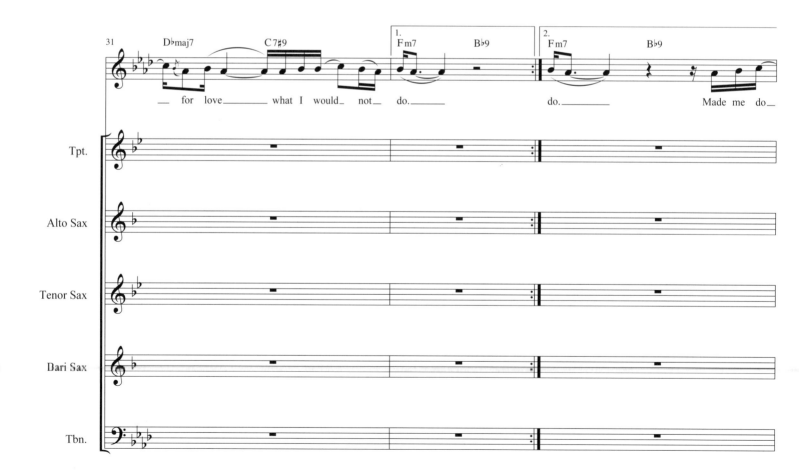

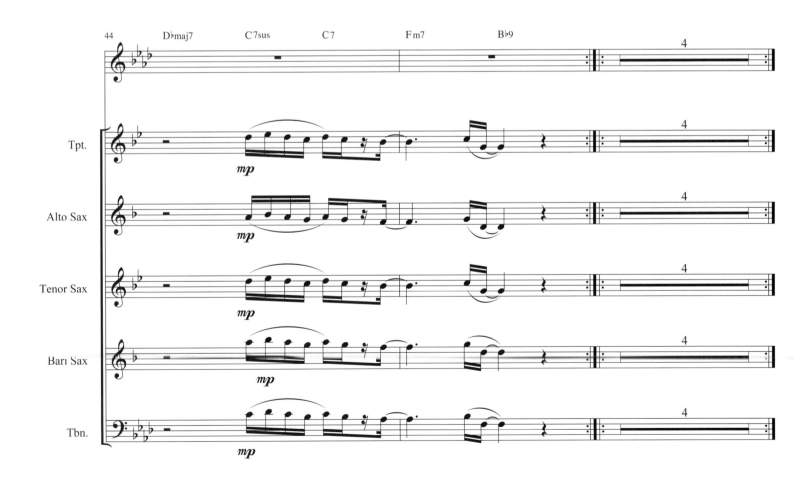

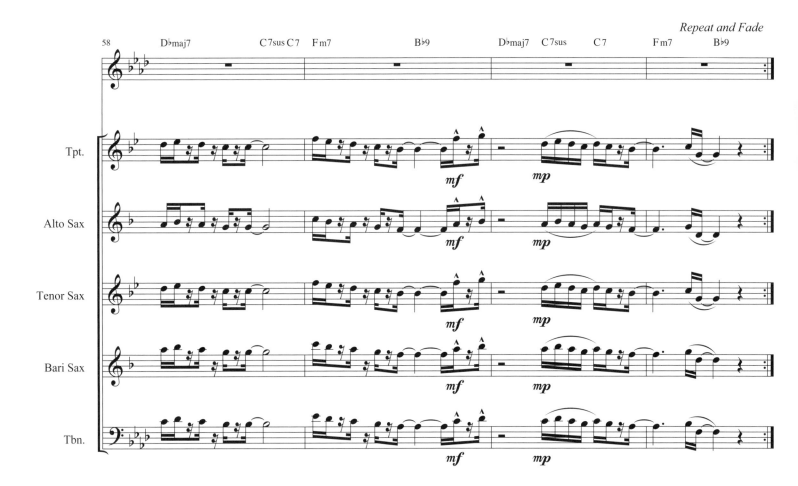

YOU CAN'T GET WHAT YOU WANT
(TILL YOU KNOW WHAT YOU WANT)

Words and Music by
JOE JACKSON

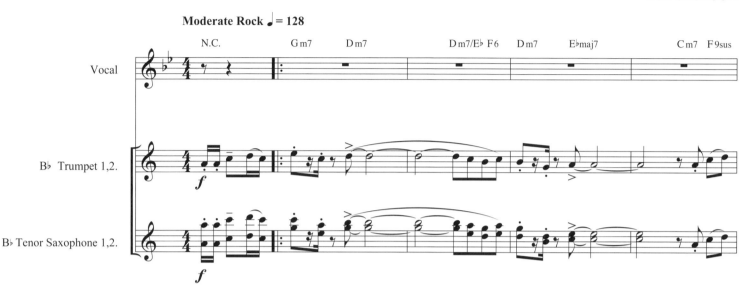

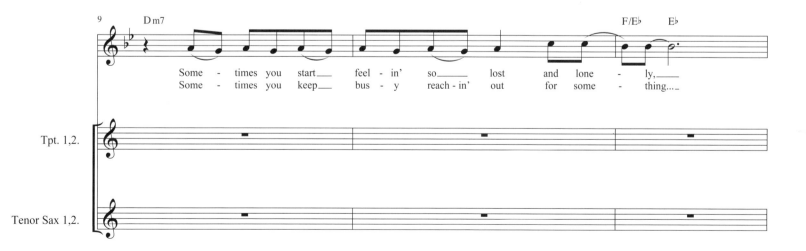

Some - times you start___ feel - in' so___ lost and lone - ly,___
Some - times you keep___ bus - y reach - in' out for some - thing....___

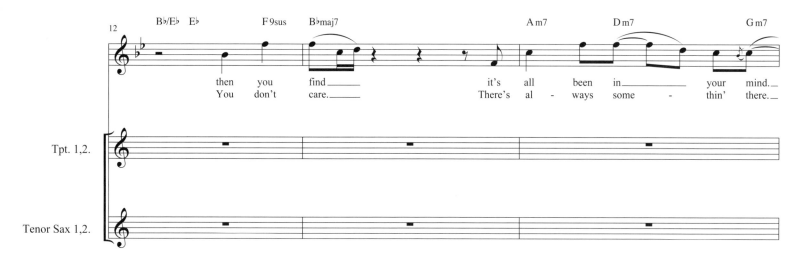

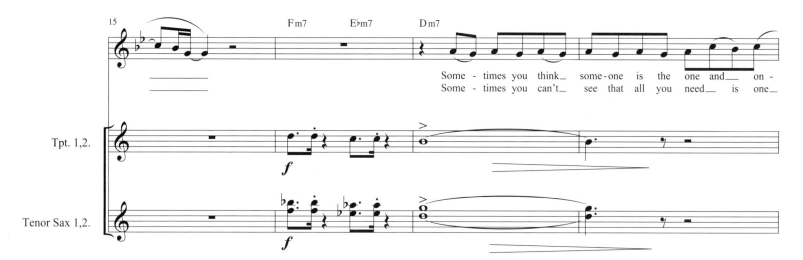

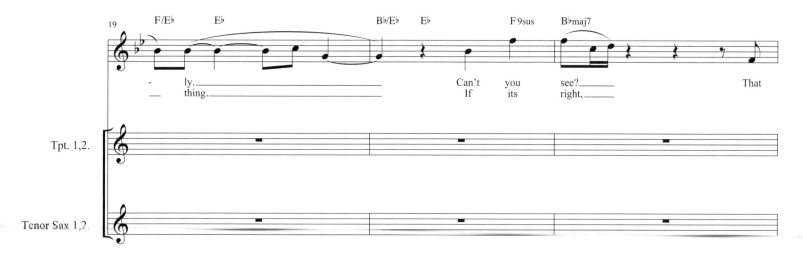

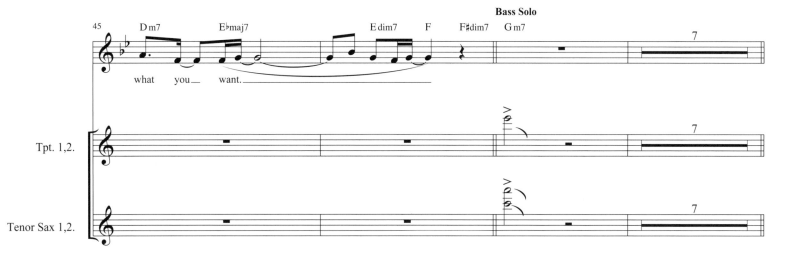

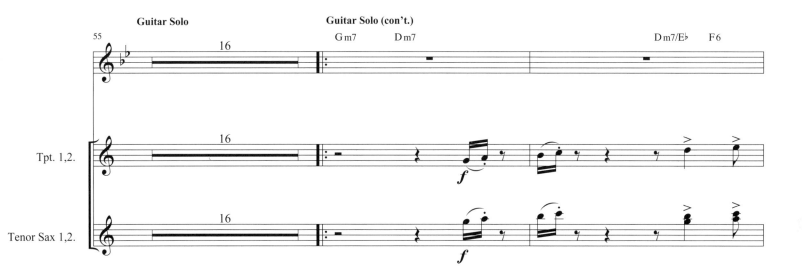

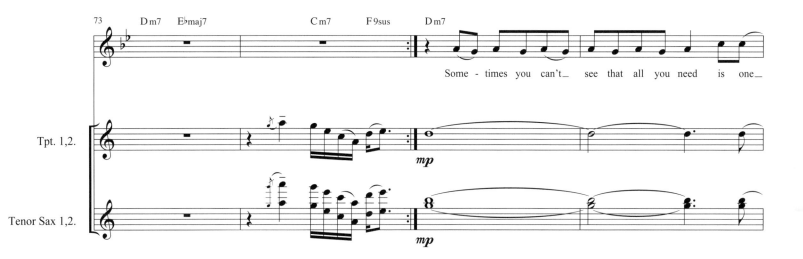

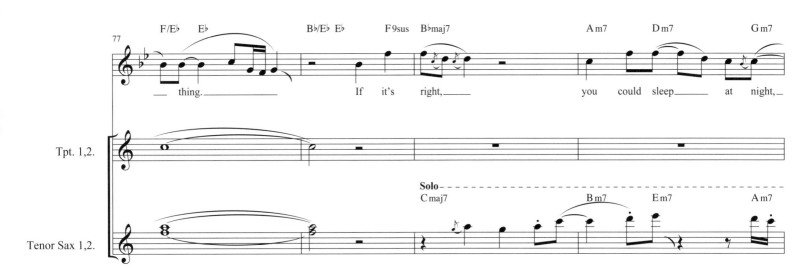

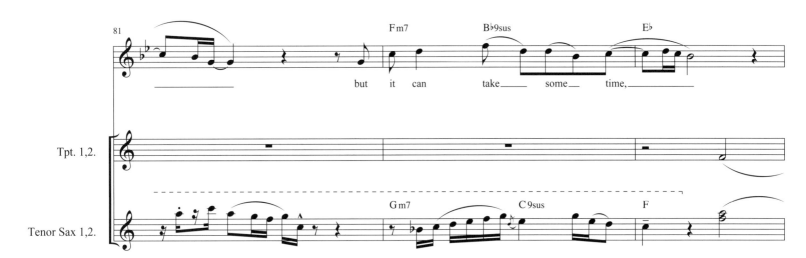

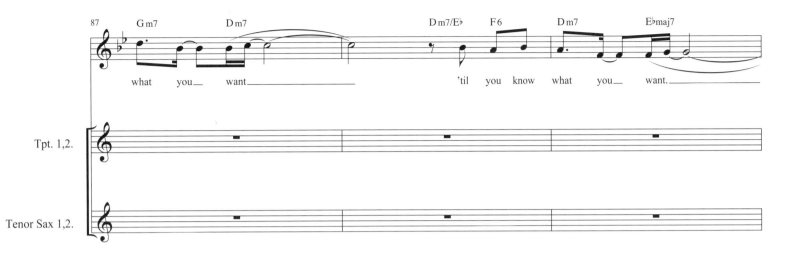

what you___ want_____ 'til you know what you___ want._____

___ 'Said you can't get what you___ want_____ 'til you know what you___ want_____

Repeat 3 times

(what you___ want.)___
(Lead vocal ad lib 2nd and 3rd times)

mf

mf

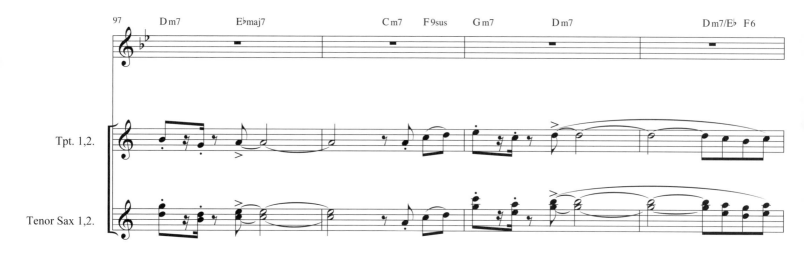

I can tell you one thing, you can't get___

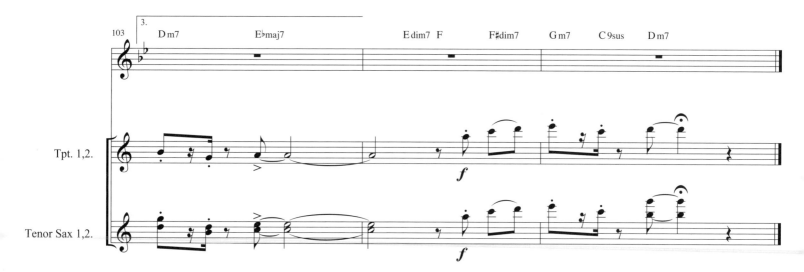

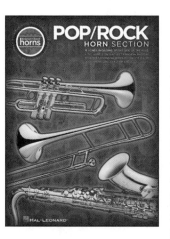

Transcribed Scores are vocal and instrumental arrangements of music from some of the greatest groups in music. These excellent publications feature transcribed parts for lead vocals, lead guitar, rhythm, guitar, bass, drums, and all of the various instruments used in each specific recording session. All songs are arranged exactly the way the artists recorded them.

00672527	Audioslave	$24.95
00673228	The Beatles – Complete Scores (Boxed Set)	$85.00
00672378	The Beatles – Transcribed Scores	$24.95
00673208	Best of Blood, Sweat & Tears	$19.95
00690636	Best of Bluegrass	$24.95
00672367	Chicago – Volume 1	$24.95
00672368	Chicago – Volume 2	$24.95
00672452	Miles Davis – Birth of the Cool	$24.95
00672460	Miles Davis – Kind of Blue (Sketch Scores)	$19.95
00672502	Deep Purple – Greatest Hits	$24.95
00672427	Ben Folds Five – Selections from Naked Baby Photos	$19.95
00672428	Ben Folds Five – Whatever and Ever, Amen	$19.95
00001333	Getz/Gilberto	$19.99
00672540	Best of Good Charlotte	$24.95
00672396	The Don Grolnick Collection	$17.95
02500361	Guns N' Roses Greatest Hits	$24.95
00672308	Jimi Hendrix – Are You Experienced?	$29.95
00672345	Jimi Hendrix – Axis Bold As Love	$29.95
00672313	Jimi Hendrix – Band of Gypsys	$29.95
00672397	Jimi Hendrix – Experience Hendrix	$29.95
00672500	Best of Incubus	$24.95
00672469	Billy Joel Collection	$24.95
00672415	Eric Johnson – Ah Via Musicom	$24.95
00672465	John Lennon – Imagine	$24.95
00672478	The Best of Megadeth	$24.95
02500424	Best of Metallica	$24.95

00672541	Pat Metheny Group – The Way Up	$19.95
02500883	Mr. Big – Lean into It	$24.95
00672504	Gary Moore – Greatest Hits	$24.95
00690582	Nickel Creek – Nickel Creek	$19.95
00690586	Nickel Creek – This Side	$19.95
00672545	Nickel Creek – Why Should The Fire Die?	$19.95
00672518	Nirvana	$24.95
00672403	Nirvana – In Utero	$24.95
00672404	Nirvana – Incesticide	$24.95
00672402	Nirvana – Nevermind	$24.95
00672405	Nirvana – Unplugged in New York	$24.95
00672466	The Offspring – Americana	$24.95
00672501	The Police – Greatest Hits	$24.95
00672538	The Best of Queen	$24.95
00672400	Red Hot Chili Peppers – Blood Sugar Sex Magik	$24.95
00672515	Red Hot Chili Peppers – By the Way	$24.95
00672456	Red Hot Chili Peppers – Californication	$24.95
00672536	Red Hot Chili Peppers – Greatest Hits	$24.95
00672422	Red Hot Chili Peppers – Mother's Milk	$24.95
00672551	Red Hot Chili Peppers – Stadium Arcadium	$49.95
00672408	Rolling Stones – Exile on Main Street	$24.95
00672360	Santana's Greatest Hits	$26.95
02500283	Joe Satriani – Greatest Hits	$24.95
00672522	The Best of Slipknot	$24.99
00675170	The Best of Spyro Gyra	$18.95
00675200	The Best of Steely Dan	$19.95
00672521	Best of SUM 41	$29.95
00675520	Best of Weather Report	$18.95

Prices, content, and availability subject to change without notice.

0212